DATE DUE

Mononucleosis

by Gustav Mark Gedatus

Consultant:
Catherine Dolan, MD
Riverside Family Physicians, Minneapolis

Perspectives on Disease and Illness

LifeMatters
an imprint of Capstone Press
Mankato, Minnesota

LifeMatters books are published by Capstone Press
818 North Willow Street • Mankato, Minnesota 56001
http://www.capstone-press.com

Printed in the United States of America

Library of Congress Cataloging-in-Publication Data
Gedatus, Gustav Mark.
     Mononucleosis / by Gustav Mark Gedatus.
         p.   cm. — (Perspectives on disease and illness)
     Includes bibliographical references and index.
     ISBN 0-7368-0284-3 (book). — ISBN 0-7368-0294-0 (series)
     1. Mononucleosis Juvenile literature. I. Title. II. Series.
     RC147.G6G43   2000
     616.9′25—dc21   99-32904
                                              CIP

Staff Credits
Kristin Thoennes, Rebecca Aldridge, editors; Adam Lazar, designer; Kimberly Danger, photo researcher

Photo Credits
Cover: PNI/©Ida Wyman, bottom; ©DigitalVision, left, right; ©Rubberball, middle
FPG International/©Barbara Peacock, 40; ©Telegraph Colour Library, 26
Index Stock Photography/11, 14, 45
Photo Network/©Phyllis Picardi, 7
PNI/©DigitalVision, 46, 58
Unicorn Stock Photos/©Deneve Feigh Bunde, 39; ©Eric R. Berndt, 17; ©Tom McCarthy, 30, 34
Visuals Unlimited/©Fred E. Hossler, 23; ©G. Musil, 8; ©Jeff Greenberg, 49, 55, 56; ©SIU, 20, 35; ©WHICH, 29

Table
of Contents

Chapter Overview

Infectious mononucleosis also is called the kissing disease, mono, or the sleeping disease.

Mononucleosis is passed through saliva.

Symptoms of mononucleosis include fatigue, sore throat, and swollen glands.

Mononucleosis attacks the immune system, causing unusual changes in some white blood cells.

Chapter 1

What Is Mononucleosis?

Dayanne, Age 16

Dayanne woke up in the middle of the night. She was very warm and her head was throbbing. She didn't sleep well for the rest of the night. The next day, Dayanne was exhausted. She assumed she was getting a cold.

By the end of the school day, the glands under Dayanne's jaw hurt and seemed swollen. It hurt for her to turn her head. Swallowing seemed difficult, too.

Dayanne's dad insisted that she go to the doctor. The doctor did a blood test. She called Dayanne later and told her that she had mononucleosis.

What Is Mononucleosis?

Infectious mononucleosis is commonly called mono. It also is known as the kissing disease. In some cases, it has been called the sleeping disease because it makes people extremely tired. Mono is passed through saliva during oral contact such as kissing. Sharing personal items such as drinking glasses or toothbrushes can spread it, too. People can get the disease from germs in the air when someone coughs or sneezes, but this rarely happens.

At least half of teens entering college are estimated to have had the disease. Many of them may not know they ever had mono because the symptoms were not severe. They probably thought they just had a bad cold.

The Epstein-Barr Virus

The Epstein-Barr virus (EBV) causes 9 out of 10 mono cases. EBV is one type of herpesvirus. Other herpesviruses can cause chicken pox, mumps, cold sores, or fever blisters. EBV attacks the immune system, which helps the body fight germs and infection.

The immune system includes the blood and the different parts of the lymphatic system. The lymphatic system is made up of vessels that drain lymph, or extra fluid, from the body's cells. Lymph glands in the neck, armpits, and groin work to keep a balanced flow of lymph.

When viruses enter the body, the immune system works to fight them off. Some cells in the blood, called white blood cells, create antibodies that fight the invading germs. These antibodies do daily battle against all sorts of different invaders. Without the immune system, the body could not survive.

EBV first infects and reproduces in the salivary glands. Then EBV begins to affect the blood. White blood cells, called B-cells, begin to reproduce in an unusual manner. Many of these cells look unusually large under a microscope. The other white blood cells, called T-cells, then are activated against the virus and destroy the damaged B-cells.

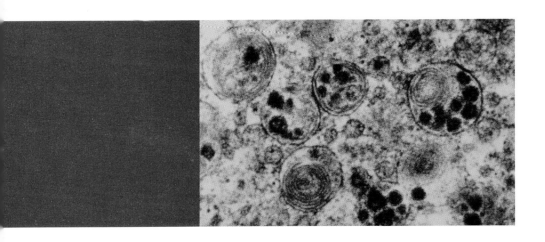

EBV attacks the lymphatic system through the blood. The lymph glands become swollen. As the immune system weakens, the body is less able to fight off disease. With the passage of time, however, a normal immune system can fight off the invading virus.

Symptoms of Mononucleosis

Early symptoms of mono may include general fatigue, headache, loss of appetite, and painful, puffy eyes. These symptoms may lead to a sore throat as well as swollen lymph glands.

A fever caused by mono may be as high as 105 degrees. In some people the fever may remain for only a few days. In others it may last for up to three weeks. A slight pink rash may develop in people with mono. Sometimes people who have mono can have a temporarily enlarged spleen. The spleen is an organ of lymph tissue that filters the blood. It also produces disease-fighting white blood cells.

In children, mono usually produces either mild flu-like symptoms or none at all. The symptoms of mono are more severe in older people.

Less common symptoms of mono are jaundice, or yellowed skin, and extreme sensitivity to light. A few people may have severe neck stiffness, a cough, or shortness of breath. There also are recorded cases of older people who had chest pain and a rapid heartbeat.

A typical case of mono lasts about two weeks. The tiredness, however, may last up to three months. Usually mono is more of an inconvenience than anything else.

Who Gets Mono?

Anyone can get mono at any age. More than 7 out of 10 people who get mono, however, are between ages 15 and 30. Doctors estimate that 50 out of 100,000 Americans have symptoms of mono at any given time. The figures are even higher for college students.

People in the United States most commonly get mono between ages 15 and 17.

Epidemics can occur at certain places at specific times. Doctors have noticed clusters of mono outbreaks. For instance, one college campus may report several cases, yet another campus may report hardly any. Doctors see most people with mono in spring and fall. However, no one knows why people get mono in one season instead of another.

Craig, Age 17

Craig never gets sick. He has not missed one day of school since the fifth grade. He eats well and gets plenty of rest. Each afternoon he plays basketball for at least two hours.

One morning Craig just didn't have the energy to get out of bed. His body seemed to hurt all over. He didn't have a cough. He didn't vomit. He just didn't feel like moving. A few days later, he had a very sore throat, too. Craig went to the doctor and found out he had mono.

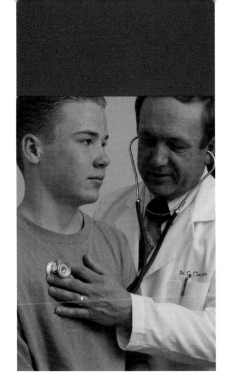

Incubation Period

An incubation period is the time from exposure to a disease to the development of symptoms. For adults exposed to mono, it may take between four to six weeks for symptoms to develop. In children and adolescents, it may take only 7 to 14 days.

Points to Consider

How do people get mono?

What are the symptoms of mono?

What is the name of the virus that causes mono?

Why do you think mono is so contagious?

Where does EBV first enter the body?

Chapter Overview

Illnesses resembling mono were recorded in the 1800s.

The term *infectious mononucleosis* came into use in the 1920s.

The study of Burkitt's lymphoma led to a better understanding of mono.

In the 1960s, Doctors Epstein and Barr identified the virus that causes mono.

Most college students who are tested already have been exposed to EBV.

Chapter 2

The History of Mononucleosis

The year was 1960. Phillip was a tenth grader at Central High. He was an excellent

Phillip, Age 16

student and a pretty good athlete, too. He had never been sick, except for minor colds and flu when he was young.

One day Phillip woke up with a sore throat. His throat was so swollen that he could hardly swallow. Later that day, Phillip's doctor told him he had mono. The doctor also told him not to worry. Phillip found out that he was not alone. Many other students had been sick with mono. Why hadn't he heard about it before?

Doctors now know a lot more about mono than they did in 1960. Now they know that a virus causes it. It is easily passed through saliva. People who get it are not unclean. Lots of average people get it.

The Beginnings of Mono

Early cases of an illness that resembled mono were recorded in the 1800s. People had swollen glands, fever, and sore throat. This disease became known as glandular fever.

Two American doctors investigated this sickness in 1920. Doctors Sprunt and Evans took blood from college students who had mono-like symptoms. The doctors found that the blood samples had a very high number of particular white blood cells. These cells were called mononuclear lymphocytes. They were larger than normal white blood cells. The name infectious mononucleosis came to describe the disease we know today. The virus that causes this disease produces the unusual mononuclear cells.

Doctors today refer to mono as a self-limiting viral disease. Self-limiting diseases are those that go away without many complications. Viral diseases are those caused by viruses and passed from person to person.

An Unusual Testing Method

In 1932, American Doctors J. R. Paul and W. W. Bunnell studied the mono virus. At that time, researchers had begun to do tests with animal blood. They often found that antibodies of one species could be used to test other species. The doctors combined blood from people with mono with sheep's blood. As seen under a microscope, the human blood clumped when mixed with animal blood. This test has been perfected and is used today for diagnosing mononucleosis. It is called the monospot test.

A Discovery Through Cancer Research

For many years, researchers tried to find out what caused mono. They conducted experiments with animals. Many experts believed that a virus caused mono, but they had no proof. Then, in the 1960s, researchers discovered something important.

Denis Burkitt was a surgeon working in Uganda in 1961. Uganda is a country in west central Africa. Burkitt found that many African children were getting a tumor of the jaw. This condition became known as Burkitt's lymphoma.

Fast Fact

Four out of ten Americans have been exposed to EBV by age five.

The children with Burkitt's lymphoma all lived in specific areas. It seemed that certain temperatures or amounts of rainfall made a difference. Burkitt believed that the climate was influencing the virus.

Burkitt sent samples of the tumor tissue to England for examination. Three researchers, M. A. Epstein, Y. M. Barr, and B. G. Achong began looking for some sort of cancer. They studied the tumor samples under a microscope. In 1964, the men identified a new form of the herpesvirus. It was named after Epstein and Barr. The two doctors determined that the virus contributed to Burkitt's lymphoma. The virus also caused infectious mononucleosis and, in rare cases, some other diseases.

Studies of College Students

During recent years, researchers have learned more about mono by studying college students. Dr. James Neiderman conducted one study of men who entered West Point Academy in 1969. Upon their arrival at school, 6 out of 10 had mono antibodies in their blood. By the time the class graduated in 1973, 8 out of 10 had the antibodies. Similar tests were done during the 1980s with comparable results.

Mimi sat with her friends on the school lawn. Her friend Gary had gotten a soft drink. He passed it around the group. Everyone took a sip. Mimi didn't like doing that, but she went along with the group.

Mimi, Age 16

"I would feel really stupid to say I can't share the drink. It's not like I haven't done that lots of time before," Mimi thought to herself. She took a swallow when the drink got to her. A few weeks later Mimi had mono. Did she get it from sharing the soft drink? She will never know for sure.

Points to Consider

When did people first start using the term *infectious mononucleosis?*

How did Doctors Epstein and Barr happen to identify the virus that causes mono?

What is Burkitt's lymphoma?

How is animal blood used to test for mono?

What statement could you make about college students and mono?

Chapter Overview

Doctors may use a complete blood count (CBC) to test for mono.

The most common test for mono is the monospot test.

Once the body has been exposed to a virus, it takes a while for antibodies to develop.

Occasionally the effects of mono on the blood may be mistaken for other diseases such as hepatitis or leukemia.

Chapter 3

Diagnosing Mononucleosis

Many of Tratnia's friends had had mono. **Tratnia, Age 17** She had been coughing a lot, and her throat felt kind of sore. At the end of the school day, she thought she had a fever.

Tratnia went to the doctor. Whenever she went to the doctor, she was afraid. All of those needles and instruments made her very nervous. The doctor was calm and thoughtful. The blood test for mono was easy.

Much to Tratnia's surprise, she did not have mono. She had a plain old head cold.

Did You Know? The younger the person, the milder the symptoms of mono.

Analyzing the Blood

The person's blood sample is mixed with the red blood cells of a sheep or horse. If the blood clumps together, the heterophile antibodies are present in the person's blood. This indicates the presence of EBV.

Frightening Confusions

Sometimes mono can be confused with other more serious diseases. The mononuclear cells of mono may be mistaken for leukemia cells. Leukemia is a cancer of the white blood cells. Fatigue and abnormal, or unusual, substances in the liver can be confused with hepatitis. Hepatitis is an inflammation, or swelling, of the liver. This disease causes jaundice and fever.

In some cases, additional tests are done to rule out these more serious diseases. For instance, upon careful examination, cells affected by mono look very similar to one another. Blood cells of people with leukemia are much more varied in appearance. Chemical evidence of mild hepatitis appears in 9 out of 10 people with mono. However, mono rarely leads to viral hepatitis and the possibility of long-term liver problems.

Chapter 3

Diagnosing Mononucleosis

Many of Tratnia's friends had had mono. **Tratnia, Age 17** She had been coughing a lot, and her throat felt kind of sore. At the end of the school day, she thought she had a fever.

Tratnia went to the doctor. Whenever she went to the doctor, she was afraid. All of those needles and instruments made her very nervous. The doctor was calm and thoughtful. The blood test for mono was easy.

Much to Tratnia's surprise, she did not have mono. She had a plain old head cold.

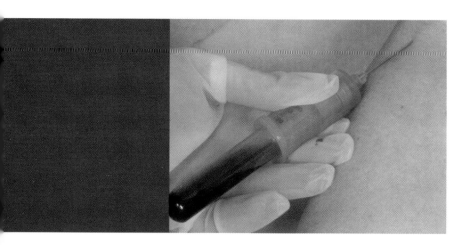

The Complete Blood Count

One test for the diagnosis of mono is the complete blood count (CBC). This test measures the number of red and white blood cells. Mono increases the number of white blood cells. It increases the number of blood cells made up of lymphocytes. Many of these lymphocytes may look abnormal under a microscope. The CBC is not as commonly used as the monospot test, however.

The Monospot Test

People who have EBV may produce antibodies known as heterophile antibodies. A monospot test, also called a heterophile test, can detect whether these antibodies have been produced.

For the monospot test, a lab technician draws blood from a vein. Usually, the technician chooses the inside of the elbow or the back of the hand. First the puncture spot, or the place where the needle will be inserted, is wiped with antiseptic. This substance kills germs and prevents infections. A tight rubber strip or blood pressure cuff is then placed around the upper arm. This applies pressure and restricts the blood flow through the vein being punctured. This causes veins below the strip or cuff to fill with blood. The needle is then put into the vein. Blood is collected in an airtight container. During this step, the rubber strip or cuff is removed to restore normal blood flow.

The monospot test is slightly different for infants and young children than for adults. The arm is cleaned with antiseptic and punctured with a sharp needle or lancet. A lancet is a sharp-pointed surgical tool used for cutting. The blood is collected in a small glass tube, onto a test strip, or in a small container. A bandage may be applied to the arm to control bleeding.

Analyzing the Blood

The person's blood sample is mixed with the red blood cells of a sheep or horse. If the blood clumps together, the heterophile antibodies are present in the person's blood. This indicates the presence of EBV.

Frightening Confusions

Sometimes mono can be confused with other more serious diseases. The mononuclear cells of mono may be mistaken for leukemia cells. Leukemia is a cancer of the white blood cells. Fatigue and abnormal, or unusual, substances in the liver can be confused with hepatitis. Hepatitis is an inflammation, or swelling, of the liver. This disease causes jaundice and fever.

In some cases, additional tests are done to rule out these more serious diseases. For instance, upon careful examination, cells affected by mono look very similar to one another. Blood cells of people with leukemia are much more varied in appearance. Chemical evidence of mild hepatitis appears in 9 out of 10 people with mono. However, mono rarely leads to viral hepatitis and the possibility of long-term liver problems.

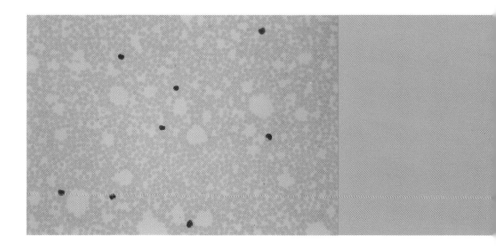

Possible Need to Retest

Keep in mind that after exposure to mono, it takes a while for antibodies to develop. Many doctors do not test for mono during the first week of illness for two reasons. The test may not turn out positive yet. Also, treatment for mono is the same as treatment for most common viruses. That includes rest, fluids, and medicine to control pain. The doctor may repeat the test in a few weeks. At this point, it should be 85 percent accurate.

Points to Consider

Which test for mono is used most often?

How are blood tests given to children?

Why might a test for mono not be accurate?

How do you think someone would feel if his or her mono cells were confused with hepatitis or leukemia cells?

Chapter Overview

Some people get over mono faster than others do.

Doctors recommend bed rest, plenty of liquids, and saltwater gargles.

People recovering from mono must be aware of the danger of physical contact while the spleen is enlarged.

Most mono symptoms cannot be treated effectively with drugs.

Chapter 4

Managing Mononucleosis

Carrie found out she had mono. She knew that her vacation with her cousins was **Carrie, Age 17** coming up in two weeks. She wasn't worried, though. Her friend, Bill, had gotten over his mono in two weeks. She was sure she would, too.

Carrie wanted to get better—and fast. She stayed in bed all day and night. She drank lots of orange juice. She gargled with saltwater. After two weeks, her fever was almost gone. Unfortunately, Carrie was still so tired that she could hardly stand up. Now she was really depressed. Her cousins went on vacation without her.

Recovery Rate

Everyone recovers from mono at a different rate. Some people have symptoms of mono for two weeks. Others might have symptoms for six weeks. It can help to do the right things in order to speed up recovery. In many cases, however, mono just has to take its course. It may be two weeks or even two months before a person feels normal again.

Common Doctors' Advice

Doctors recommend that people with mono lessen their activity for two to three weeks. For most people this is a natural thing to do, because mono usually makes people feel very tired. Swollen, sore lymph glands in the neck often accompany mono. Sitting up to read or even watch TV can be difficult. Lying flat in bed often is the most comfortable position for the neck.

The fever with mono usually is not above 102 degrees. However, in some people it briefly may get as high as 105 degrees.

People who drink plenty of liquids can help mono to pass through their body. Mono is one of many diseases that causes dehydration, or loss of water. Therefore, it is important to replace moisture that the body loses during the illness.

A sore throat may make people with mono uncomfortable. It can make swallowing difficult. To recover quickly, people need to keep eating nutritious foods. Vitamins and minerals from good food help the immune system to do its work.

There are different ways to relieve a sore throat. Some people gargle with saltwater. Others drink plenty of cool liquids.

Taking Care of the Spleen

The spleen is the organ that filters blood. It also produces disease-fighting white blood cells. The spleen is located in the upper left-hand side of the abdomen. Mono sometimes results in a tender and enlarged, or bigger, spleen. Sometimes the liver is affected, too. Doctors recommend that people with mono limit their movements. Physical contact, especially sharp blows to the body, can cause a puncture, or hole, in an enlarged spleen. This is also known as a ruptured spleen. If left untreated, the person could die from blood loss.

In some cases, the spleen may remain enlarged after other symptoms have disappeared. It can still be fragile. Contact from the shoves and jabs of sports such as football may still be dangerous. Doctors have different opinions about how soon athletes can return to vigorous activity after having mono. Usually, it takes an athlete three to six months to get back into top form after having mono.

Medications for Mono

No drug eliminates mono from the body. Medications do not help most symptoms of mono. In some cases, however, mono may lead to other infections that require medicine. For instance, a strep infection sometimes complicates mono. Strep is a sore throat that is caused by bacteria. It can be treated with antibiotic drugs that kill bacteria. Unfortunately, sometimes when the strep thoat is treated with certain antibiotics, the person with mono can get a rash.

People who have severe symptoms of mono are sometimes treated with prednisone. This drug can reduce fever and shrink swollen glands. Sometimes it makes swallowing easier, which improves the appetite. This drug works in extreme cases, but it is not recommended for everyone. This is because prednisone can cause many unwanted side effects.

Terrence got mono in September. He missed the first two weeks of school.

Terrence, Age 17

When he went back, he felt funny. It seemed like the other students had a head start. Terrence was glad that his sore throat and swollen glands were better. He worked hard to make up for lost time in school.

In the middle of October, Terrence started feeling really sick again. He felt like his lungs were filled with fluid. His mom told him she thought his mono had returned. Terrence went back to the doctor. He found out that his immune system was still weak. He had an infection, but his mono had not returned.

Mono—Again?

After you have mono, it may take months before you feel completely normal. Sometimes you may feel tired just because you are depressed about having been sick. When you are sick, you miss out on some things. Rest assured, however, that mono does not return. Once you have had it, you will not get it again.

Nine out of ten people with mono who take ampicillin for a strep infection get a skin rash.

Fast Fact

Points to Consider

How long does mono last?

What steps should someone take to recover from mono?

Do you think it would be difficult for a teen to follow a doctor's advice for treating mono? Why or why not?

Why is it important for people with mono to avoid contact sports?

How do medications affect the symptoms of mono?

Chapter Overview

Rupture of the spleen among people with mono can result in death if left untreated.

Some people have a weakened immune system that cannot fight EBV.

There is no known connection between mono and chronic fatigue syndrome.

EBV sometimes leads to hepatitis or blood disorders such as leukemia or anemia.

Chapter 5

Rare Health Problems Related to Mononucleosis

Ruptured Spleen

In healthy people, the spleen seldom ruptures. A serious accident can cause a rupture, but under normal circumstances ruptures do not occur. This is true even of vigorous sporting activity. However, people with mono are different from healthy people. Many people with mono have an enlarged spleen that may or may not cause any pain. When the spleen is enlarged it is more vulnerable, or likely to be hurt.

EMERGENCY

Eric had a sore throat and swollen glands for a few weeks. He felt out of it for a while. When the doctor told him he had mono, it was no big deal. Lots of his friends had lived through it.

Eric, Age 18

Eric often played touch football before he got sick. When he finally was feeling better, he joined his friends for a game. At one point, someone lightly tackled him and he fell on the ball. Later that afternoon, Eric had a horrible pain in his side. His dad called the paramedics. That night, Eric had emergency surgery to remove his spleen.

Eric was feeling better in a few weeks. The doctors said he had probably ruptured his spleen while playing ball. Without the surgery, Eric could have bled to death.

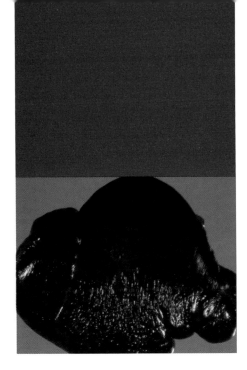

When the spleen is punctured, the person feels a sharp pain in the abdomen. This is the part of the body between the chest and hips. The person may feel light-headed, have a rapid heartbeat, or have difficulty breathing. The puncture causes uncontrolled internal bleeding. Surgery is necessary in all cases. Unless the damaged spleen is removed, the person will die.

Most people who have mono do not get a ruptured spleen. In fact, fewer than 1 out of 1000 people with mono gets this dangerous condition. However, avoiding physical contact while recovering from mono is a wise precaution. Sports such as football can be especially hazardous if the spleen is enlarged.

Fast Fact

In some cases, mono can lead to extremely severe inflammation of the tonsils.

A Disabled Immune System

Some people have a weakened immune system that cannot fight EBV. The lymph nodes progressively enlarge and lymphomas develop in these people. Lymphomas are tumors of the lymph glands. Sometimes antibody production is permanently affected in a negative way. This very rarely happens. These conditions usually result in death.

Most diseases caused by EBV are usually found in people with weakened immune systems. For example, people who have had organ transplants take special drugs. These drugs help the body to accept the new organ. Unfortunately, these drugs also cause a weakening of the immune system. As a result, tumors of the lymph glands may develop.

Myth: People of some races are more likely to get mono than others.

Fact: No race of people is more likely to get mono than any other is.

Unusual Blood Disorders

In some rare cases, a doctor may decide to check the person's bone marrow to rule out leukemia. That means the doctor needs to check the soft substance inside of the bone. If a person has leukemia, it does not necessarily have any connection to an earlier case of mono.

In very few mono cases, the person's blood count is seriously changed. The number of white blood cells, red blood cells, or platelets may be greatly reduced. Platelets help the blood to clot. One common type of change is anemia. People with anemia have a decrease in the number and volume of red blood cells.

Fast Fact

There are eight known types of human herpesviruses. There are many more in the animal world. The herpesvirus that leads to mono is EBV.

Inflammatory Diseases

At times, hepatitis, meningitis, and encephalitis have been associated with mononucleosis. Of these conditions, hepatitis is the most common, especially in older adults. Meningitis and encephalitis are inflammations of parts of the brain or spinal cord. These diseases can result in seizures or convulsions. Both can be fatal. However, none of these diseases is a common outcome of mononucleosis.

Anna had mono when she was only 13. She had a sore throat and a fever. She also had very little energy. Even when she was getting better, she seemed tired all the time.

Anna, Age 17

Anna still gets tired very easily. In fact, she often passes up invitations to go out because she is just too tired. Anna thinks that she tires easily because years ago she had mono.

Fatigue

Some people believe that the tired feeling from mono does not go away. This is not true. If a person has constant fatigue, there is some other medical problem. Perhaps the person has insomnia, or lack of sleep. Perhaps the person's blood is low in iron.

In the past, there have been some experts who believed that EBV caused chronic fatigue syndrome in some people. People with chronic fatigue syndrome feel tired all the time. It may last for months or even years. EBV can cause fatigue in people who get mono, but this tiredness is usually short-lived. Most doctors believe there is no proven connection between EBV and chronic fatigue syndrome.

Temporary Complications

Sometimes other diseases complicate mono. These illnesses may be painful and bothersome, but they are not permanent. For instance, myocarditis can complicate mono. Myocarditis is an inflammation of the heart muscle. A person with mono also may have ataxia, or difficulty with muscle coordination. This can make it hard for the person to perform simple physical tasks. He or she may have trouble just walking in a straight line.

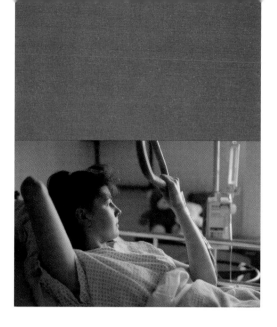

One type of paralysis has been connected to mono in unusual cases. In this temporary crippling condition, some or all of the person's muscles may be unable to move. This condition usually passes, but it can leave the person very weak for a long time.

Some people who get mono may have a fever even after other symptoms have ended. A small group of people may have fatigue that lasts longer than normal. Both conditions are rare and usually pass with time.

The Rarest Cases

In a few cases, very young people with mono have had serious complications. They may have inflammation of the sac around the heart. This is called pericarditis. They could have inflammation of the brain, or meningitis. Their red blood cells could be destroyed.

Points to Consider

What happens when a person's spleen is punctured?

Why do people who have had organ transplants have a weakened immune system?

How are encephalitis and meningitis alike?

What would you say to someone with chronic fatigue syndrome who said it came from having mono?

Chapter Overview

Resting in bed, drinking liquids, and gargling with saltwater can help people with mono to recover.

Complete recovery from mono may take a while.

Mono is a temporary illness.

Part of recovery includes positive thinking about getting on with your life.

People understand more about mono than ever before.

Chapter 6

Living With Mononucleosis

People may feel that they are over mono in a few weeks. Usually that means that the sore throat and swollen glands are gone. Complete recovery, including having your energy back, can take a couple of months. In some ways, this may be the hardest part of having mono. It requires patience.

Myth: If you live with someone who has mono, you will get it.

Fact: You might not. Mono is passed through saliva. In 1997, a test of college roommates was done. Roommates of people with mono picked up the virus no more easily than others in school.

Ginnie thought she had strep throat. She went to the doctor for a throat culture, or

Ginnie, Age 16

test. The doctor suggested a monospot test. It turned out that Ginnie had mono. She missed about three weeks of school. She spent most of that time in bed. She was able to keep up with some of her schoolwork at home.

A month later, Ginnie's family went on vacation. She had been back in school for a while and felt pretty well. However, when her family went mountain climbing, Ginnie couldn't keep up. "What's wrong with you, Ginnie?" asked her brother. "You are usually racing ahead of everyone."

"I guess my mono is not really gone," said Ginnie. "I just don't have my usual energy." Ginnie had fun on vacation, but not as much fun as usual.

Taking Care of Yourself

You have read about the importance of bed rest. You know that drinking lots of fluids is a good idea. Saltwater gargles can help soothe a sore throat. You may even want to suck on Popsicles or eat sherbet or ice cream. The cold will ease the throat pain and swelling.

Bed rest also gives a fever time to pass. By avoiding strenuous exercise, you will not make a fever even higher. Also, cutting out vigorous activities decreases the chance of damage to your spleen while you recover.

Nonaspirin pain relievers such as ibuprofen or acetaminophen may help relieve the sore throat and fever of mono. Many doctors believe that aspirin should be avoided. In some cases, it has been known to cause Reye's syndrome, an illness occasionally associated with mononucleosis.

In some cases, a strep infection may complicate the sore throat of mono. If this happens, a doctor can prescribe antibiotics. These drugs can help limit the pain of throat discomfort. They also can help limit how long it lasts. More importantly, these drugs help to prevent rheumatic fever. This is a serious disease that causes fever, joint pain, and possible heart damage.

Your State of Mind

You may have to miss a big dance because of mono. Perhaps your date was somebody you like a lot. Will he or she end up going with someone else? Will there be another big date for the two of you?

Perhaps you have become an important part of an athletic team. What will happen to your involvement while you are in bed with mono? Will you lose ground on the team after all your hard work?

I thought that I could at least watch TV or read. Every time I tried to do either of those things, I felt even worse! I got a headache and my neck seemed even stiffer.
—Ellen, age 13

Maybe you are close to graduating. How will you ever get your diploma if you can't take the tests? How can you take the tests without making up all the work you missed while you were sick?

For years, you may have wanted a good after-school job. Now you have that job. Then you get mono. What will happen? Will the boss think that you are someone who can't be counted on?

These are just a few of the possible situations you may face as you recover from mono. Sickness never happens at a convenient time. Something gets missed. Something else gets delayed. Mono interrupts your life.

Depression is a common partner to illness. You may feel like there are some losses you will never recover. Being alone in bed may make you feel lonely or isolated. You may feel trapped. Each hour, each day may seem to take forever to pass.

Mono does pass. In the meantime, it presents a real challenge. Frustration is common for people who get sick. You will find, however, that patience can make recovery easier.

You may feel like friends ignore you while you are sick. You think that maybe they are afraid of catching mono. Maybe you think they just don't care. Perhaps they just don't know what it's like. They are busy with their own lives. Your friends may simply be allowing you time to rest and even sleep. If any of your friends get mono, you will know how to be a friend to them.

Coping With Mono

If you have mono, only you can decide how effectively you will deal with it. Family members and friends can help, but getting over it is really your own effort. If you get mono, you can do these things to cope with your illness:

Follow doctor's orders.
Your doctor knows what is best for you. Make sure to listen to his or her recommendations and to follow them.

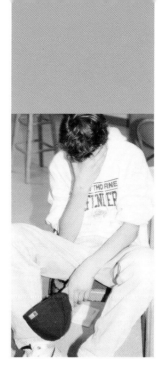

Give yourself good self-care.

Get a lot of bed rest, and drink plenty of liquids. If you have a sore throat, gargle with saltwater often.

Avoid strenuous activity.

Too much activity before you're ready can make you feel more tired. It also can put your spleen at risk.

Have a good mental attitude.

The illness eventually will get better. Keep that in mind. Make a list of things that you want to do when you are well. Doing so might help to raise your spirits.

Take it slow.

Be patient with your body. If you find that you don't have all of your energy back, rest. Give the recovery process a little more time.

I felt like the earth opened up and I just fell in. I thought I would never get better. But you know what? I did. It only took about three weeks.
—Sophia, age 15

Le was new to his school. He was still learning English. He didn't feel like he fit in at all.

Le, Age 16

When Le got mono, he knew it wasn't from kissing. He hadn't been kissing anyone.

Le missed almost a month of school. When he did go back, he felt like even more of an outcast. He was really depressed.

Katarina, who also was new, organized a little party for Le. It was a belated Welcome-to-America party. Le met a lot of other kids. Many of them told him that they, too, had dealt with mono.

Points to Consider

What are some physical things you can do to take care of yourself if you have mono?

Why should you not take aspirin if you have mono?

If you have had mono, what was the most difficult aspect of it? If you have not had it, what do you think would be the hardest part?

In your opinion, what is the most important thing someone can do for his or her state of mind during mono?

Chapter Overview

Researchers have difficulty finding a suitable animal model for mononucleosis research.

Some monkeys carry a virus similar to EBV.

Researchers hope to learn even more about the immune system.

Perhaps new virus-fighting T-cells can be created.

Australians may have discovered a vaccine for mono.

Chapter 7

Looking Ahead

Coreena is thinking about becoming a doctor. She doesn't want to be a regular doctor with patients. She wants to get a medical degree for research.

Coreena, Age 18

"If I were a medical researcher, I would first focus on diseases like mono," she told a group of friends. "I know it's a lot more popular to work on AIDS or cancer or heart problems. But mono touches the lives of many people, too. Maybe I feel like it's sort of an easy one to work on first. After mono is taken care of, I can concentrate on other diseases."

At least 7 out of 10 Americans have been exposed to EBV by the time they reach age 20.

Mono Research

Researchers have tried using animals to study mono. Experiments with EBV in mice have been somewhat successful. However, mice are not similar enough to human beings. Scientists' findings were limited. Researchers found that animal primates could not become infected with EBV. Animal primates are groups that include monkeys and apes. It appeared that no suitable animal model ever would be found.

Scientists discovered that some rhesus monkeys carry a certain virus. This virus is similar to EBV. The virus was transmitted to a different group of monkeys. Researchers studied the blood of these monkeys before and after infection. They found dramatic changes in the blood cells of the monkeys. These changes were not unlike the effects in humans. Scientists hope to gain more knowledge of this virus in monkeys. In doing so, they may develop valuable new knowledge about the human virus.

Difficulty in Battling EBV

Researchers know that EBV produces many different kinds of antigens. In fact, it produces more than 100 types of these particles that cause a response from the immune system. The body's white blood cells combine with the antigens and kill viral cells. As a result, healthy people are able to recover quite quickly from mono. Understanding the different kinds of antigens may help lead to a vaccine against mono in the near future.

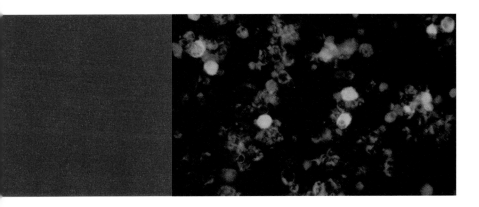

When mono is associated with lymphoma or some cancers, only
one kind of antigen is produced. T-cells in blood are unable to
combine with this antigen. Without this combination, infected
cells cannot be attacked. The virus is able to hide from the body's
immune system. Many such diseases are life threatening. In some
cases, two treatments for cancer, called chemotherapy and
radiation, can help control damage to the body. Scientists hope
that new learning will lead to development of different aids for
the human immune system.

In developing nations, 9 out of 10 children under age 5 have EBV in their blood but have no symptoms.

Jackson had mono when he was only 14. **Jackson, Age 18** It really was not so bad. He felt tired and he had a sore throat. He stayed home from school for a couple of weeks. When he was 18, he needed a physical for joining the football team. After a blood test, the doctor told him that he tested positive for mono

"Hey, what gives? When I was 14, I had mono. The doctor I had then told me I wouldn't get it again? Was he wrong?" Jackson wanted to know.

The antibodies for fighting mono show up in the bloodstream. They remain there long after symptoms have ended. In some people, they stay there for their entire life. Jackson did not have mono a second time. However, the antibodies continued to appear in his blood test.

Some mono is spread by people who had it years ago. Experts believe that more than 1 out of 10 people transmit mono for decades after they get it themselves. The average person with mono can pass it through saliva for about 18 months after getting it.

A Vaccine Against EBV

Researchers in Australia may have the answer to preventing mono. At the Australian Queensland Institute of Medical Research, a vaccine is about to be tested on human volunteers. Researchers hope that the vaccine will help the body to produce additional T-cells. At this point, researchers know that the vaccine is not harmful to people. They do not know how successful it will be. Until a vaccine for mono is found, many young people will have to deal with it.

Points to Consider

Why have researchers had trouble using animals to study mononucleosis?

What difficulties do researchers have in fighting EBV?

Would you volunteer to test a possible vaccine for mono? Why or why not?

Glossary

antibody (AN-ti-bod-ee)—proteins that the body produces to help fight disease and infection

antigen (AN-ti-juhn)—any substance allowed into the body that causes production of an antibody

antiseptic (an-ti-SEP-tik)—a substance that kills germs and prevents infection by stopping the growth of germs

chronic (KRON-ik)—lasting for a long time

convulsion (kuhn-VUL-shuhn)—an involuntary jerking movement of the muscles or the whole body

dehydration (dee-hye-DRAY-shun)—not having enough water in the body

enzyme (EN-zime)—a protein in the body of humans and animals that causes chemical reactions to occur

Epstein-Barr virus (Ep-STEEN BAR VYE-ruhss)—a herpesvirus that causes most cases of mono

hepatitis (hep-uh-TYE-tis)—inflammation of the liver

herpesvirus (HUR-peez-VYE-ruhss)—any of several viruses that may cause chicken pox, mumps, cold sores, fever blisters, mono or other diseases

incubation (ing-kyoo-BAY-shun)—time from exposure to a disease to development of symptoms of that disease

leukemia (loo-KEE-mee-uh)—cancer in which blood makes too many white cells

lymph (LIMF)—a clear liquid containing some white and red blood cells that runs through the body and carries away waste

lymphocyte (LIM-fuh-site)—a white blood cell formed in the lymph nodes or spleen

rupture (RUHP-chur)—to break open or to burst

For More Information

Harris, Jacqueline L. *Communicable Diseases.* Breckenridge, CO: Twenty-First
    Century Books, 1995.

Hyde, Margaret O., and Elizabeth H. Forsyth. *The Disease Book: A Kid's Guide.*
    New York: Walker, 1997.

Silverstein, Alvin, Virginia Silverstein, and Robert Silverstein. *Mononucleosis.*
    Springfield, NJ: Enslow, 1997.

Smart, Paul. *Everything You Need to Know About Mononucleosis.* New York:
    Rosen, 1998.

Useful Addresses and Internet Sites

American Medical Association
515 North State Street
Chicago, IL 60610

Centers for Disease Control and Prevention
1600 Clifton Road NE
Atlanta, GA 30333

National Institute of Allergy and Infectious
Diseases
National Institutes of Health
Office of Communications and Public Liaison
Building 31, Room 7A-50
31 Center Drive MSC 2520
Bethesda, MD 20892-2520

Laboratory Centre for Disease Control, Health
Canada
Tunney's Pasture, Postal Locator 0603E1
Ottawa, ON K1A OL2
CANADA

American Academy of Family Physicians
http://www.aafp.org/patientinfo/mono.html
Offers information on getting through
mononucleosis

Health Resource Directory
http://www.stayhealthy.com
Provides many links to health and wellness
resources about mononucleosis

U.S. Food and Drug Administration
http://www.fda.gov/fdac/features/1998/
398_mono.html
Offers article for teens about mononucleosis

KidsHealth
http://www.kids.edu/parent/common/
mononucleosis.html
Gives general information on mononucleosis

Index